For Your Garden

CITY GARDENS

For Your Garden
CITY GARDENS

WARREN SCHULTZ

Little, Brown and Company
Boston New York Toronto London

First Edition

ISBN 0-316-77597-5

Library of Congress Catalog Card Number 94-77516

A FRIEDMAN GROUP BOOK

10 9 8 7 6 5 4 3 2 1

Published simultaneously in Canada by Little, Brown & Company (Canada) Limited

FOR YOUR GARDEN: CITY GARDENS
was prepared and produced by
Michael Friedman Publishing Group, Inc.
15 West 26th Street
New York, New York 10010

Editor: Kelly Matthews
Art Directors: Jeff Batzli and Lynne Yeamans
Layout: Philip Travisano
Photography Editor: Susan Mettler
Production Associate: Camille Lee

Color separations by Fine Arts Repro House Co., Ltd.
Printed and bound in China by Leefung-Asco Printers Ltd.

Table of Contents

INTRODUCTION

In the midst of steel, glass, and asphalt, a city garden often seems more than a luxury; it can be a necessity. City dwellers revel in the soft and comforting sight of green and take care to sprinkle lush doses of it throughout the urban landscape. It doesn't take much—certainly large expanses of land and huge expenditures of time and money can be avoided.

At the same time, however, a city garden can contain nearly everything held dear by its boastful country cousin. Deep in the heart of a city, gardens can be built around trees and shrubs and proudly show off bulbs, annuals, and perennials. Designs can be formal or casual, and it's not beyond the realm of a city garden to produce vegetables and fruit. In fact, the concept of edible landscaping took root in the city, where gardeners and landscapers realized that food crops could add beauty to the landscape as well as produce a bountiful harvest.

The city garden is, by nature, intensive and efficient. It makes the most use of a small space. Entering an urban oasis, one often feels engulfed by greenery and swept away from the hustle and bustle of the city. At the same time, city gardens present a challenge, because they must be precise. It's vital that plants match the surroundings. The qualities that make successful city gardens are the same as those that mark poetry and art: a sense of harmony, rhythm, and surprise. These elements open your eyes and allow you to see things in a new light.

OPPOSITE: What a delight to wake to breakfast in the garden. This patio's lush environment is provided almost entirely by potted plants. They seem to draw the vines, shrubs, and trees from the background closer, creating the feeling of dining in the wilderness.

ABOVE: Framed with vining greenery, this formal courtyard is highlighted with flowering annuals and perennials. A careful mix of foliage and flowering plants arranged with just enough open space to feature the flagstone floor, it's a delightful secret garden to view from ground level or from a bird's eye.

ABOVE: City gardens may be planned to be seasonal sensations. The corner of this courtyard is designed to shine in the spring when rhododendrons burst into flower. It's ready and waiting for the gardener who is eager to spend some time outside after being cooped up all winter.

OPPOSITE: It's vital for all the elements in a city garden to work together. Many of the best highlight hardscape embellishments, such as this chimney pot planted with marjoram. The cobblestones are another important feature in this circular patterned garden, as they make room for the integrated beds of herbs.

ABOVE: City gardens can be intensely planted patches of nature. This water-wise planting in the southwestern United States mimics a prairie or wildflower meadow and completely transforms an ordinary square plot.

OPPOSITE: In the midst of hustle and bustle, a city garden provides an oasis of green, a peaceful Shangri-la. Brimming with blooming plants both in the ground and in pots, this courtyard is also blessed with a little patch of turf.

ABOVE: A front-door garden may bring together very different elements. This sprawling yellow-flowered rose is complemented by the potted plants at its feet. Without the tulips, geraniums, and other blooms, the bare base of the climbing plant might appear awkward. The terra-cotta containers serve to draw the eye when the plants are not blooming.

OPPOSITE: The classic cottage garden suits virtually any city situation, even the entry to a modern condominium. Paving stones lead the way through this mixed planting of traditional perennials and native plants, and the overriding feeling of wildness and disorder is toned down by the surrounding picket fence.

ABOVE: A shady corner of a patio is the perfect setting for a Sunday brunch. Climbing vines soften the effect of these adobe walls, while potted plants provide spots of color.

OPPOSITE: Attention to detail makes even the most obscure corner of garden space grand. Here, the clipped box plants draw attention to the lion's-head fountain, but their reduced height also allows the water garden to take center stage. White flowering snowflakes along the wall provide a delicate counterpart to the stonework.

OPPOSITE: Formal city gardens can be quite successful when they focus on greenery and highlight just a few flowers. Here, framed by well-groomed hedges, roses are the stars, with the geometric hedge pattern designed to direct the visitor around and through the paths.

ABOVE: Tiny aboveground city gardens can make large statements. With its carefully combined and designed plantings of pansies and hyacinths, this single window box certainly qualifies as a garden that makes its presence known.

ABOVE: A good garden creates a sense of place—and there's no doubt that this front yard takes up residence in the southwestern United States. The intense sunlight and brightly painted woodwork give the location away. The cheery daffodils seem at home in their terra-cotta pots, where they can be watered on a daily basis and moved out of the parching sun if necessary.

OPPOSITE: The best city gardens fit in with their surroundings, while the most exciting ones also attempt something daring. Here, cacti, succulents, and palms combine with wildflowers to present a desert cottage garden. By using low-water natives, this city garden requires little maintenance and is less subject to disease.

Chapter One

THE SECRET GARDEN

Many of the most memorable city gardens offer the much-desired element of seclusion. A courtyard not visible from the street, a rooftop hidden by vines, a terrace shrouded in greenery—all are tiny enclaves of privacy. These hidden gardens sustain urban gardeners, surrounding city green thumbs with their own patch of nature.

Secret gardens, however, can be the most difficult to design and maintain. On patios, terraces, and rooftops, and in empty lots and even alleyways, the conditions are often not entirely hospitable, and the gardener has to search out the right plants for the environment. Most often, city gardens are lost in shade, so their success often relies heavily on such tough, shade-tolerant plants as hosta, impatiens, begonias, ivy, and azaleas. At the same time, scented plants, night-blooming vines, shrubs, and small trees should be considered. Choose plants that aren't finicky, and include a sampling of plants that look good through all four seasons.

As with any garden, the first task in building the secluded city garden is to examine the advantages and shortcomings of the site, making sure the basic needs of plants can be provided. There's nothing sadder than a few scraggly bushes or dying vines looming over your patio. They'll need sunlight—at least six hours a day for most plants. And don't forget water or the ability to deliver it. Drip-irrigation systems are ideal for secret gardens because these systems themselves can be hidden. You may also have to bring soil into the garden. You can buy bales of soil-less mix or simply amend the soil with peat moss and compost.

Lastly, don't forget design. A city garden can be a diverse and changing scene by including early spring bulbs, summer annuals, and autumn perennials. Also, to help maintain privacy, include vines and small shrubs. And there should be little nooks and crannies for tables, benches, chairs, or perhaps even a hammock for hiding away with a good book.

ABOVE: Treasured assets, city gardens are designed to be used frequently, often as outdoor rooms. In fact, a city garden would hardly be a garden without an enticing seat or bench. Here, it would be difficult to resist stopping to smell the roses climbing behind this lovely slatted bench.

OPPOSITE: Bright colors, bold lines, and straightforward designs are the hallmark of American southwestern art. Here, the garden is centered around a mosaic pool, with a potted plant serving as a simple focal point.

OPPOSITE: A dense planting of perennials completely surrounds and insulates this patio garden. The aged patio bricks bring an instant touch of history to this urban setting.

ABOVE: Although directly across the street, the brownstones that neighbor this empty-lot oasis seem miles away. The juxtaposition is quite dramatic as the plants impart a tropical feeling to an inner-city environment. This city garden works miracles, transporting the gardener and visitors alike and imposing its renewing greenness on the surroundings.

ABOVE: Up on the roof, nature doesn't feel so far removed if you can bring a little bit of greenery with you. Here, scattered potted plants, long flower-box "borders," and trellises work to create a suburban backyard feeling on this city roof.

OPPOSITE: If not for the "boardwalk," you could easily get lost in this rambunctious city garden. Birch trees, broad-leaved cannas with their bold flowers, and all manner of vines and foliage plants nearly obscure the surrounding buildings and provide a secluded hideaway.

OPPOSITE: Sometimes city gardens are conceived, designed, and built for one reason: to provide shade-blessed respite. Here, a deck becomes a delightful spot to dine, but only because it's protected from the sun by surrounding trees. Potted plants also appreciate the break from the otherwise unrelenting sunshine.

ABOVE: Daylilies, rudbeckia, *Echinacea*, and *Liatris* are all common elements in the type of formal border that you would expect to find on a British estate. Here, the same plants are packed onto a city roof, creating an intensified garden with concentrated color.

ABOVE: Gardens in the city can serve to soften the harsh lines and stark colors of modern architecture. This gardener has cleverly combined varying plant heights and forms to bring dimension to the flat vertical surface behind.

ABOVE: Early in the season with the trees just beginning to bud, enough sunlight penetrates this courtyard garden to allow blooming bulbs and azaleas to dominate. Later, the trees will cast a deep shade, and foliage plants will become the main features.

RIGHT: Simple, understated edge plantings combined with brightly colored garden furniture suit this town house patio. In addition to adding punctuation points of color, the container plants also help to soften and incorporate the angular pool with its green surroundings.

OPPOSITE: The wise city gardener knows when to rein in plants to let the hardscape shine. Plantings here are kept low and somewhat subdued so as not to compete with the architecture of the coach house and octagonal terrace.

ABOVE: Where there's room, the symmetry of a circular garden is especially enchanting in the city. Surrounded by straight lines and corners, the circle emphasizes the softer, flowing elements of a garden. A bench at the perimeter beckons visitors, and the sundial in the center serves as a focal point.

ABOVE: An urban garden can make a striking statement without a single flower. This rooftop deck is edged by a great variety of foliage plants in various hues of greenish gray and silver. The cool, subdued effect they produce succeeds in enhancing the modernness of the structure.

OPPOSITE: Sometimes a single tree can serve as the centerpiece of a city garden. Anchored by a willow-leafed pear, this bulb border serves to frame a sharply edged lawn.

ABOVE: The tall, straight forms of hollyhocks and sunflowers superbly mirror the vertical lines of the skyline behind them. In fact, at dusk, the skyscrapers may appear to be nothing more than shadows thrown by the flowers in the foreground.

OPPOSITE: City gardens are often designed as sanctuaries. Even in the midst of a congested urban area, they provide a peaceful place for relaxation. Here, vines and vertical plants soften the brick walls and add more of a buffer from street noise. There's a chair tucked in among the plants, but it would be tempting to stretch out on the manicured patch of lawn.

Chapter Two

THE WELCOMING GARDEN

*S*ome city gardens are meant to be seen and enjoyed by all. Planted along a sidewalk, in a front yard, or by a doorway, welcoming gardens are designed to entertain and catch the eye of passersby. They're often colorful, playful, exuberant. The front-door garden is also an ideal place for highlighting forms and shapes as well as colors. Keep in mind, however, that these plantings will set the tone for the rest of the landscape, and therefore, care must be taken to match plants and garden designs to a building's architecture.

The front-door garden is often easier to maintain than the more hidden backyard garden, because it is usually smaller and often in a sunny spot. On the other hand, its exposure to curious eyes makes it subject to daily scrutiny, so the gardener must be prepared to spend time grooming the area, removing spent flowers, pulling weeds, raking, pruning, and trimming.

The styles of welcoming city gardens can be as different as the gardeners tending them. They may be formal perennial borders, casual annual beds, cottage gardens, window boxes, container gardens, or even patches of wildflowers along the sidewalk.

In fact, just about anything goes in front of city homes these days. Gone are the days of uniformity, when every front lawn looked identical and residents sought anonymity. Gardeners now are daring to be different, expressing some personality and individualism in their front yards. And the urbanscape is the better for it.

OPPOSITE: An entry garden can offer plenty of colors, textures, and types of flowers. To take advantage of different growing conditions, rhododendrons have been planted here in the foreground shade, with potted tulips in the sunny areas by the door. Vines and hanging plants complete the scene.

ABOVE: The wooden fence that bisects this dooryard garden creates new possibilities for plants. Providing a sense of symmetry and balance, plantings have been placed on both sides of this dividing structure, thereby helping to physically separate the house from the walkway, while at the same time uniting these two elements aesthetically.

ABOVE: With closely planted sun-loving summer bloomers such as roses and geraniums tumbling over the front walkway, this tiny, overflowing cottage garden creates a dramatic entry to this town house. Wandering through this mass of color, visitors may feel as though they've left the city for the countryside.

OPPOSITE: Sometimes simplicity conveys elegance. Urns potted with simple white flowers are all it takes to extend a warm welcome in this stately doorway while still maintaining a sophisticated tone in keeping with the building's architecture.

OPPOSITE: Flower beds placed around the perimeter of this front courtyard soften the tiled surface, while the black metal obelisks provide vertical interest and support for climbing plants. The patio gives the garden a spacious feeling, but also beckons visitors to step inside the gate and take a leisurely tour of the garden.

ABOVE: A potted topiary is the focal point for this front-door planting. The tree stands subtly in the shade while climbing plants and vines first attract streetside attention. The topiary will come as a pleasant surprise to visitors as they approach the door to ring the bell.

ABOVE: Nothing brightens and cheers an entryway as effectively as a hanging planter. It's an enchanting way to hang out a welcome sign and let folks know that you take pride in your surroundings.

OPPOSITE: A solitary, majestic hollyhock stands like a sentinel beside this front door, draping and cradling the vestibule. A hanging basket provides a splash of deep color.

ABOVE: Some front-yard gardens make their mark by being disciplined and understated. Here, a rope-twist terra-cotta edging defines the borders of a well-ordered garden. The mix of ground covers and flowering plants is highlighted by a square of Corsican mint lawn.

OPPOSITE: A garden following the slight bend of front steps greets visitors and draws them along the low incline to the front door. Foliage plants provide the canvas while potted flowering plants add warm color.

ABOVE: Window boxes, urns, hanging baskets, and pots provide a plethora of fertile ground for bright begonias, impatiens, lobelia, and other plants. This garden produces a riot of front-yard color that's surely famous throughout the neighborhood for its nonstop vibrant blooms.

OPPOSITE: It's important to keep the front garden concordant with other architectural elements in a setting. Here, there's no question that the terra-cotta and slate quarry-tile walkway makes a bold play for attention, but instead of planting it with competing colors, the gardener relies on foliage plants for a perfect accompaniment.

ABOVE: A nondescript corner on the front of a city dwelling can be improved considerably by a window box. This box adds dimension to the otherwise vacant space, but the gardener plays it cool with subdued colors.

OPPOSITE: In stark, dignified surroundings, simple classic flowers in bold colors make a refined impression.

Chapter Three

EDIBLE CITY GARDENS

ortunately, ownership of a country estate isn't a mandatory requirement for growing fruits and vegetables. There's room in almost all city gardens for a few edible plants. In fact, food plants are often asked to perform double duty in smaller gardens. Lettuce, for example, may be selected and grown for the color and texture of its leaves as well as for its flavor. Sprays of tiny tomatoes can be as ornamental as any flower, and vining crops can be grown up elaborate trellises and in hanging baskets.

And don't forget fruit. Fruit trees can be espaliered or trained against fences for an elegant look. Or they can be allowed to grow as a centerpiece of a garden or be interplanted with a ground cover or understory of flowers. Bushes, such as blueberries or gooseberries, can be used as hedges. Vines, including grapes and kiwis, can be planted as well.

When planting a city food garden, raised beds, rich soil, and mulches are often a must for healthy plants. Also consider mixing plant textures and colors for creating interesting designs and patterns. It's fun to experiment with plant combinations, such as lettuce with nasturtiums or carrots with marigolds. Succession planting is also advised so that the garden is always producing.

There's nothing like being able to step outside to pick fresh herbs or harvest a few tomatoes and serve them still warm from the sun. And luckily, the edible landscape is easily and uniquely adaptable to an urban setting.

RIGHT: The humble pumpkin can have quite an artful impact when transported to a small plot of city land. There are also many new compact varieties of pumpkins, squashes, and other vine crops that will grow in bush form, making them suitable for small spaces.

OPPOSITE: The wide variety of low-growing, well-behaved herbs makes these plants an important ingredient in the formal city garden. Their leaf colors range from silver to gray to purple and include every shade of green from chartreuse to emerald. Learn how to identify the species and you can design a unique small garden.

ABOVE: All of the most popular crops, including tomatoes and peppers, can be grown in pots in small city spaces. Potted plants may need some special care, however, such as extra watering. Staking and tying may also be necessary to prevent them from tipping over, because even normally compact plants such as peppers may grow extra tall in city conditions.

OPPOSITE: There's no rule that says vegetables and flowers can't be mixed. Here, the deep, dark color of waxy cabbage leaves adds a decorative touch to this wooden trough that few ornamentals could provide. The purple hues combine perfectly with the nasturtiums and French marigolds.

ABOVE: Close, intensive planting is a hallmark of city food gardens. Here, all the makings of a fine salad—lettuce, leeks, onions, herbs, cucumbers—are crowded into a small raised bed. The tight spacing is also effective for shading the soil and crowding out weeds.

LEFT: Some vegetable plants are natural trailers or climbers and can be grown in the unlikeliest places to take advantage of their natural growth tendencies. All you need is a hook and a hanging basket in a sunny spot to produce a copious crop of cucumbers.

RIGHT: Virtually any vegetable can be grown in a container— sometimes to its benefit. This artichoke plant might have a hard time producing fruit in the cool ground of a northern garden, but when potted, it can be easily moved to the sunniest, most protected areas. As it is, the plant contributes a glorious gray-green foliage to accent its companions.

BELOW: Even when squeezed into a tiny spot and forced to get by on a sparse ration of sunlight, many vegetables will still produce. Although this pepper plant has to stretch for the light, it still pumps out a good harvest.

ABOVE: The best way to introduce edibles into a city situation may be the herb garden. To start cultivating herbs simply and quickly, consider a thyme bed. Here, various types of thyme offer a wide range of colors, shapes, and textures.

OPPOSITE: Herbs are well suited to container life. As shown here, they can be planted and trained even in the smallest spaces to grow in intricate patterns and designs.

Chapter Four

GARDENS WITHOUT GROUND

Even if you have only a doorstep or window ledge, there's still space enough for a garden. Give the dedicated gardener a pot, and he or she will grow anything from pansies to green beans to roses, shrubs, or a peach tree.

The beauty of a container garden in the city is its mobility. If the sun won't shine on the garden, the garden can go to the sunshine, thus overcoming the common problem of shade cast by buildings and fences in the city. A container garden can also provide an ever-changing show by spotlighting flowering plants as they bloom and moving others into the wings as they wait for their time in the sun.

Container plantings work best when pots and plants are grouped together to make a harmonious statement. They may grow a little better too, because a grouping of plants will keep the humidity higher. A little extra care may be required for container plantings. They need loose, porous, but moisture-retentive soil and very frequent watering. While planning your container garden, make sure you can get water to the plantings easily. If watering is a hassle, you won't do it as often and your garden will turn out to be an eyesore instead of a visual treat.

OPPOSITE: Just about anything can be grown in containers. Sometimes, the fancier the container, the more inspired the plantings. Here, a jardiniere from the 1950s is planted with lacecap hydrangea while a miniature potted hedge grows below.

ABOVE: The best container plantings start, naturally enough, with the container. Here, an elegantly aged urn sets the tone for this effusive planting of marigolds, verbena, and geraniums. This design presents an ideal balance between upright and trailing flowers.

OPPOSITE: Brick, stone, and concrete steps are natural accompaniments for city gardens, and they work well with potted plants. Here, the terra-cotta of the pots echoes the brick, and the different levels of steps are used to a great advantage to add depth to the planting.

ABOVE: It's sometimes amazing how many blooms one plant can produce. This rhododendron is virtually overflowing with early spring bloom. A plant of this size and vigor needs plenty of water and fertilizer to keep it going.

ABOVE: When it comes to outdoor container gardens, most gardeners plant flowers, but it doesn't have to be that way. Foliage plants, such as these ferns and hostas, can be made to feel right at home in pots.

OPPOSITE: Here's the ultimate container: a patio water garden. The shallow pool holds water-loving plants and is replenished by water flowing from the lion's-head fountain. Potted geraniums ease the transition from water garden to patio.

ABOVE: In the city garden, buildings and walls are inevitable features. It's best if they don't intrude on the landscape but allow flowers, such as these lilies and herbs in containers, to shine.

RIGHT: Sometimes, simplicity is best when it comes to city plantings. A mix of vibrantly colored petunias filled in with trailing vinca makes a classic planting. The petunias will also provide a lovely scent.

OPPOSITE: Large terra-cotta tubs form the focal point of this city garden. Planted with striking topiaries, these tubs also feature an attractive understory of flowers that tie in with the white pansies planted in the foreground.

ABOVE: These postmodern pots prove perfect containers for miniature roses. Their simple colors and stark design catch the eye but also allow the flowers their share of attention.

OPPOSITE: Compact plants, such as ranunculus and primulas, are the best choice for small pots, such as this stone trough.

ABOVE: It's amazing how a few potted plants can transform a scene. Pots of bright, cheerful geraniums brighten this patio and create more of an outdoor feeling. Containers can also be arranged for maximum effect, surrounding a specific area and allowing the scent of the flowers to pervade.

OPPOSITE: If you like your gardens neat and orderly, containers are the way to go. If space is limited, try placing pots on tiers. Here, a wide variety of flowers is grown successfully in a very small area. From hyacinths to tulips to narcissus, bulbs grow especially well in pots and can even be forced to bloom early indoors.

ABOVE: When space is at a premium in the city, containers can make nearly any garden design possible. They're perfect for highlighting different colors, shapes, and textures of plants.

RIGHT: This brick wall serves as a perfect backdrop for a creative city garden that utilizes almost every manner of planting style. Clipped bay topiaries stand guard over the flowering bulbs in pots. There's an exotic agave in the corner and a carefully tended lawn, along with statuary, interesting pots, and vines.

INDEX

PHOTO CREDITS